Also by Lucie Brock-Broido

A Hunger

The Master Letters

Trouble in Mind

These are Borzoi Books, published in New York by Alfred A. Knopf

Stay, Illusion

Stay, Illusion

Lucie Brock-Broido

Alfred A. Knopf, New York 2015

This Is a Borzoi Book
Published by Alfred A. Knopf

Copyright ©2013 by Lucie Brock-Broido

All rights reserved. Published in the United States by Alfred A. Knopf, a division of
Random House LLC, New York, and in Canada by Random House of Canada Limited,
Toronto, Penguin Random House companies.

www.aaknopf.com/poetry

Knopf, Borzoi Books, and the colophon are registered trademarks of Random House LLC

Pages 99–100 constitute an extension of this page.

Library of Congress Cataloging-in-Publication Data
Brock-Broido, Lucie.
[Poems. Selections]
Stay, Illusion : Poems / By Lucie Brock-Broido.—First Edition.
pages cm
ISBN 978-0-307-96203-4 (Paperback)
ISBN 978-0-307-96204-1 (eBook)
I. Title.
PS3552.R6145A6 2013
811'.54—dc23   2013023978

Jacket image: The Wilton Diptych (reverse, detail). Anonymous, 14th c. © National Gallery,
London/Art Resource, NY
Jacket design by Carol Devine Carson

Published October 21, 2013
First Paperback Edition, March 2015

For My Sisters

Annie, Julie, and Melissa

CONTENTS

I

II

III

IV

Infinite Riches in the Smallest Room

Silk spool of the recluse as she confects her eventual mythomania.

If it is written down, you can't rescind it.

Spoon and pottage bowl. You *are* starving. Come closer now.

What if I were gone and the wind still reeks of hyacinth, what then.

Who will I be: a gaudy arrangement of nuclei, an apple-size gray circle

On the tunic of a Jew, preventing more bad biological accidents

        From breeding-in. I have not bred-

In. Each child still has one lantern inside lit. May the Mother not

Blow her children out. She says her hair is thinning, thin.

The flowerbed is black, sumptuous in emptiness.

Blue-footed mushrooms line the walkway to my door. I would as soon

Die as serve them in a salad to the man I love. We lie down

In the shape of a gondola. Venice is gorgeous cold. 3 December,

Unspeakable anxiety about locked-in syndrome, about a fourth world.

I cannot presume to say. The violin spider, she

Has six good eyes, arranged in threes.

        The rims of wounds have wounds as well.

Sphinx, small print, you are inscrutable.

            On the roads, blue thistles, barely

Visible by night, and, by these, you may yet find your way home.

A Meadow

What was it I was hungry about. Hunger, it is one
Of the several contraptions I can turn on the off-button to at will.

Yes, yes, of course it is an "Art." Of course I will not be here
Long, not the way the percentages are going now.

He might have been
                    Half-beautiful in a certain optic nerve

Of light, but legible only at particular
                    Less snowy distances. I was fixed on

The poplar and the dread. The night was lung-colored

And livid still—he would have my way
                    With me. In this district of late

                    Last light, indicated by the hour
Of the beauty of his neck, his face was Arabian in contour

Like a Percheron grazing in his dome of grass.

If there is a god, he is not done
Yet, as if continuing to manhandle the still lives of

The Confederate dead this far north, this time of year, each
Just a ghostly reason now. Of course there are reasons. One:

Soon the wind will blow Pentecostal with the power of group prayer.

Two: the right to bear arms. Three: he did not find my empathy
Supernatural, at the very least!

—Have you any ideas that are new?

I was fixed on the scythe and the harlequin, on the priggish
Butcher as he cut the tenderloin and

When I saw this spectacle, I wanted to live for
A moment for a moment. However inelegant it was,

It was what it might have been to be alive, but tenderly.

One thing. One thing. One thing:

Tell me there is
A meadow, afterward.

FREEDOM OF SPEECH

If my own voice falters, tell them hubris was my way of adoring you.
The hollow of the hulk of you, so feverish in life, cut open,

Reveals ten thousand rags of music in your thoracic cavity.
The hands are received bagged and examination reveals no injury.

Winter then, the body is cold to the touch, unplunderable,
                    Kept in its drawer of old-world harrowing.

Teeth in fair repair. Will you be buried where; nowhere.

Your mouth a globe of gauze and glossolalia.
And opening, most delft of blue,
                    Your heart was a mess—

A mob of hoofprints where the skittish colts first learned to stand,
Catching on to their agility, a shock of freedom, wild-maned.

The eyes have hazel irides and the conjunctivae are pale,

With hemorrhaging. One lung, smaller, congested with rose smoke.
The other, filled with a swarm of massive sentimentia.

                    I adore you more. I know
The wingspan of your voice, whole gorgeous flock of harriers,

Cannot be taken down. You would like it now, this snow, this hour.
                    Your visitation here tonight not altogether unexpected.

The night-laborers, immigrants all, assemble here, aching for to speaking,
                    Longing for to work.

You Have Harnessed Yourself
Ridiculously to This World

Tell the truth I told me   When I couldn't speak.

Sorrow's a barbaric art, crude as a Viking ship   Or a child

Who rode a spotted pony to the lake away from summer

In the 1930s   Toward the iron lung of polio.

According to the census I am unmarried   And unchurched.

           The woman in the field dressed only in the sun.

Too far gone to halt the Arctic Cap's catastrophe, big beautiful

Blubbery white bears each clinging to his one last hunk of ice.

I am obliged, now, to refrain from dying, for as long as it is possible.

For whom left am I first?

             We have come to terms with our Self

Like a marmoset getting out of her Great Ape suit.

Currying the Fallow-Colored Horse

And to the curious I say, Don't be naïve.

The soul, like a trinket, is a she.

I lay down in the tweed of one man that first frost night. I did not like the wool of him.

You have one mitochondrial speck of evidence on your cleat.

They can take you down for that.

Did I forget to mention that when you're dead

You're dead a long time.

My uncle, dying, told me this when asked, Why stay here for such suffering.

A chimney swift flits through the fumatorium.

I long for one last Blue democracy, which has broke my heart a while.

How many minutes have I left, the lover asked, To still be beautiful?

I took his blond face in my hands and kissed him blondely on his mouth.

Meditation on the Sources of the Catastrophic Imagination

Green as alchemy and even more scarce, little can be known
Of the misfortunes of a saint condemned to turn great sorrows

Into greater egrets, ice-bound and irrevocable. The wings were left ajar
At the altar where I've knelt all night, trembling, leaning, rough

As sugar raw, and sweet. From the outside, peering in, it would seem
My life had been smooth as a Prussian ship gliding on the bridegroom

Of her Baltic waters in a season of no wind. Tinny empire,

Neighborhood of Bokhara silks, were you to go, I would stop—simply
                    As a pilgrim putting down his cup. Most of my life,

I had consorted with the unspeakable, longing to put my mouth
On it. I was just imagining. I can be

Resumed. Some nights, I paint into the scene two Doves,
I being alternately one and then the other, calling myself by my kind.

                    In the living will if it says: *Hydrate.* Please.
Hydration only. Do not resume me then.

HEAT

In Belarus, the fourteen-year-olds one thin flight away

Heard Oswald singing in the shower,

In his cool American. It was 1959. In crush

They sent a note to say how sweet

A songbird he was then.

Dear Girls, he wrote, I want very much to meet you, too.

Four Novembers later not far from West Virginia, we were scooped

Back home from elementary school in rain not-quite-yet snow

To put our heads down in the mink-skin of our mothers' laps.

                              Open Carry is the law in Oklahoma now.

I just feel more safe, said Joe Wood, cocked

Among the waffles and the syrups and the diners

At the diner there. On the jukebox, Lefty Frizzell

Is singing "Long Black Veil" inside the flannel rain.

Well back beyond the Iron Curtain, I write to you tonight

From Minsk, where no child will ever cry into my lap, all seal

And cashmere, chintz. I put my eye against the peephole

Drilled so long ago through Oswald's bedroom wall

And see the leafless world all quietened.

My little gun's a Lady one. I just want to feel secure

And I'm probably dead on. I want very much

To meet you. I would be, as ever, yours.

DOVE, INTERRUPTED

Don't do that when you're dead like this, I said,

Arguably still squabbling about the word inarguably.

I haunt Versailles, poring through the markets of the medieval.

Mostly meat to be sold there. Mutton hangs

Like laundry pinkened on its line.

      And gold! —a chalice with a cure for living in it.

We step over the skirt of an Elizabeth.

Red grapes, a delicacy, each peeled for us—each sheath

The vestment of a miniature priest, disrobed.

A sister is an Old World sparrow placed in a satin shoe.

The weakling's saddle is worn down from just too much sad attitude.

No one wants to face the "opaque reality" of herself.

                    For the life of me.

I was made American. You must consider this.

Whatever suffering is insufferable is punishable by perishable.

In Vienne, the rabbit Maurice is at home in the family cage.

I ache for him, his boredom and his solitude.

On suffering and animals, inarguably, they do.

                    I miss your heart, my heart.

Dear Shadows,

If it gets any darker in here no one will ever be able to see again, like cats

With their eyes sewn shut at birth.

I could barely stand to write what I just wrote just now.

On the heavy walnut table—numbles for roasting on a truss of fire,

The loin, a spit, an iron moving in a fit of blood.

Here, sit in the lap of me and purr.

Once in the imagination's feckless luck, in the excelsior of living wild, I wore a pinafore

Of linsey-woolsey cloth—knowing he was too shy to unbutton it in back.

Miss Stein would never, not in this life, appear unto my vex of work.

What is not ever said you can't take back.

Goats slaughtered young would have made the softest gloves for him, his hands.

Pronouns are not to be trifled with, possessive ones or otherwise.

(Mine is a gazelle, of course.)

I am of a fine mind to worship the visible world, the woo and pitch and sign of it.

And all that would be buried in the drama of my going on.

SELECTED POEM

Who was I—lying in the cattails and the milkweed's flue,
In the tiny adjectival prows of leaves of sugar maples and of great

Oak trees; the burrs of newly dying things were in my hair.
A girl in gentle murder in the bowl of being there.

Nothing was rhetorical.
Everything was sepia.

It was a time when my father may have been alive.

In the Gargoyle Store, I buy a gryphon off the rack.
When I go home, I am Solange in Jean Genet's *The Maids.*

The production moves through the sooty basements of churches
Full of persons wrapped in the coppery leather limbs of methadone.

Their arms are scarified and wracked with rain.
I am still almost a virgin, technically.

I have made promises I may not keep, go on with my

Soliloquy and was some kind of beautiful.

LUCID INTERVAL

Tread very gingerly; you've used up almost all the words.

Heavy worry about growing small again, but this time accidentally.

Don't be so fanciful. If you'd add those mustard-family vegetables

To the pot roast   It would feed so many more.

                    Shepherds are still tender in a time of war.

New lovers plagiarize say awkward things and yearn.

My heart's desire would be only to desire, but not to grasp.

              And not by yonder blessed celestial anything I swear.

Of Tookie Williams

A thousand inmates' spoons for music
While the paper kite flies like a boy-weed caught

In wind from San Quentin to nestle in the next
Prison and the next. Do not do this thing,

The kite said,
But not that gently on the page of it.
No, said

The Governor, Not if Mr. Williams won't atone.
Underground, a pen of clemency will not irritate

The vellum of the night.
There was a snag, the warden said.

So enormous was Tookie's arm

The needle couldn't enter it, eleven minutes poking
There to find the vein,

Thirty-six to put him down.

Tookie was a big man,
The warden said, But it's only salt that stops

The heart—you know—that simple.

But if I say "simple" for example, I mean

That in the private gardens
Of our aristocracy, the animals are haltered in

                    Or bled out broad by
Day and when they take them down,

The children are only very gently
Sad, a habit of the class they were born to.

Me, I am not "mean," I'm told, only
Vengeful, which is a relief to me, of course.

The wind is kicking up now. Lung for lung.
                    Soon I will be done for.
On his last night here on earth, he took only milk.

For a Clouded Leopard in Another Life

You were a seed still in Darwin's left breast pocket,
Not imagined yet, almost invisible in the felt
                There just above his heart,
The bluey nubbin sleeping in a child's
                                Unmarred arms.
Things vanish in the morning when we wake
Like loam that only grows on buttermilk, at night.
In April, a tiny feline on the ledges of a billow cloud,
Or like the finch let loose in the mossery, you were ended
        Unexpectedly; what is only left of you is only me.

Pax Arcana

The Amish housemaid lived in one small room inside the lemon cookie jar

Of our mother's mother's pantry at the lake in Canada.

Her linens were chenille and bumpy, worn. Her only jewels were bobby pins.

After supper, after covering the crust of the rhubarb pie with a tea towel,

She retired early to her room. She took off her cotton cap.

She undid the hooks and eyes of her stiff black apron-dress,

Stood reading the chapter from the longsome blue-bound book.

Just as the light on the lake was dimming, at the end of days,

She snuffed out her one late wicker-shaded lamp, and lit (with a curiously

Long-reaching safety match) the waxing crescent-moon above the provinces.

> She folded her floury hands beneath her head
>
> And went to her knees by the doll-sized bed.

CONTRIBUTOR'S NOTE

What if it is true now

I do not want to speak of that

Which has been given me to say?

See, each four-legged rests his face against

The fence's slats and asks

No questions: why or how. How long.

How dare you come home from your factory

Of autumns, your slaughterhouse, weathered

And incurious, with your hair bound

Loosely, not making use

Of every single part of the horse

That was given you. What of his hooves.

His mane. His heart his gait his cello tail

His joy in finding apples fallen

As he built his coat for winter every year.

FATHER, IN DRAWER

Mouthful of earth, hair half a century silvering, who buried him.

With what. Make a fist for heart. That is the size of it.

                              Also directives from our DNA.

The nature of his wound was the clock-cicada winding down.

                              He wound down.

July, vapid, humid: sails of sailboats swelled, yellow boxes

Of cigars from Cuba plumped. Ring fingers fattened for a spell.

                              Barges of coal bloomed in heat.

It was when the catfish were the only fish left living in the Monongahela River.

Though there were (they swore) no angels left, one was stillbound in

The very drawer of salt and ache and rendering, its wings wrapped-in

                              By the slink from the strap

Of his second wife's pearl-satin slip, shimmering and still

                              As one herring left face-up in its brine and tin.

The nature of his wound was musk and terminal. He was easy

                              To take down as a porgy off the cold Atlantic coast.

                              In the old city of Brod, most of the few Jews left

Living still may have been at supper while he died.

That same July, his daughters' scales came off in every brittle tinsel color, washing

To the next slow-yellowed river and the next, toward west, Ohio-bound.

                    This is the extent of that. I still have plenty heart.

II

Extreme Wisteria

On abandon, uncalled for but called forth.

The hydrangea of her crushed each year a little more into the attar of herself.

Pallid. Injured. Wild in ecstasy. A throat to come home to, tupelo.

                              Lemurs in parlors, inconsolable.

Parlors of burgundy and sleigh. Unseverable fear.

Case history: wistful, woke most every afternoon

                              In the green rooms of the Abandonarium.

                              Beautiful cage, asylum in.

Reckless urges to climb celestial trellises that may or may not have been there.

So few wild raspberries, they were countable and triaged out by hand.

Ten-thousand-count Egyptian cotton sheets. Intimacy with others, sateen.

                              Extreme hyacinth as evidence.

Her single subject the idea that every single thing she loves

                              Will (perhaps tomorrow) die.

High editorial illusion of "control." Early childhood: measles, scarlet fevers.

Cleopatra for most masquerades, gold sandals, broken home;

Convinced Gould's late last recording of the Goldberg Variations was for her.

Unusual coalition of early deaths.

Early middle deaths as well. Believed, despite all evidence,

In afterlife, looked hopelessly for corroborating evidence of such.

Wisteria, extreme.

There was always the murmur, you remember, about going home.

POSTHUMOUS SEDUCTION

The orchard grew excellent,

Good mass of apples assembling, one angel burned, looped
On the wire fence, in a bowl of gold.

                    The animals were curiosities to most
And this was years ago. Now we do tricks for

Them, anything, for even an ersatz miracle.

                    Now, my skirt is full of briars from
                    Leaning in the late marsh grass,

A small red spider spindling in the hem (most splendidly).

                    One must keep watch over
The good doctor, ministering as he does in the darkening

Room, by the braid of light shed by the gold mass of good
                    On the barn's musty floor. Come,

Messenger in an ankle-length
Black coat, our velvet one, where once the orchard was ablaze.

Notes from the Trepidarium

At the Museum of Modern Art, she had to quit the shadow box

Of Kafka's ruin of a life; she couldn't stand the hugeous gob

Of bug emerging green beneath the metal bed.

As a child, she would never open the closet door alone

Again to choose which dirndl skirt to wear to school.

A conference of muddied seagulls would surely now be hooked

On every wire hanger mimicking the hooded crows amassed

In Hitchcock's one-room-schoolhouse yard in 1963.

Now the Eskimos are frightened at the robins in their weirdly warming

Village because their language has no word for robin—not quite yet.

A cough (small as Keats' before his brother even knew) set in.

Quit this crying out from fear in sleep; it isn't merciful.

Stop making such a racket in your wooden shoes

As you go up and down the master stairs.

MISFITS

Where I grew up in blue, before the rich red seasons of American,
                        I had thought that everything would always

                  Go our way—save Marilyn Monroe weeping

On the dry plains against the noosing
                   Of the rag of mustangs wild to keep alive

                  And the rugged craggy men who took them
Down, to sell their hooves and haunch, their meat for meat.

                I, soon to be an element of the lunatic

Fringe, am willing to kill for their right
To life: I thought the horses beautiful.

                I cringe to think I stood for nothing, for a jar
Of jam and marriages, my usage of exotic words (chimerical), my lilac apron, me

                 Starry in our own home-movie, handsome, noir
As the one dark brooding stallion, kicking going down.

In Owl Weather

In the pamphlet, on page three, you will find me

Clutching the yellow parasol, the one I used
To get away with carrying. I loved once, in

The long-ago, nesting in the empty granary
With my barn boys, all of whom then wanted

Me. How many nights it was I did not wed
Them, preferring the company of animals

Who did not speak and slept curled to me and set
Me free thereafter to the feral dark, and then

      To overwintering. In owl weather I am

Apprentice to the common law of harm.
No rook, no reed, no rain, only

Overhearing in the next room
The Surrealist's boot growing into

      The foot-soldier's missing hank

Of limb on the terrible concrete in the city
Of Tehran. This is the hour when no living

Creature can lean its forehead into my hand.
The owl in the barn is so still

No one takes my word that he is real.
In the pamphlet, on page seven, you will find me

As a tiny odalisque on the endless blanket

Of the bower of my mother's bed, coquettish,
In a poplin nightgown and my mallow-color shoes,

With all my lionlikes about me—it is clear I am
Quite pleased with me. I wonder, can he

      Look up to the slip of moon late days

At the very moment I am looking too,
I wonder, is he warm, somewhere, in hay.

Humane Farming

Come now, rain, close the eyes of the diminutive philosophers
Which are always open—foraging, inquiring, remembering
(The cruelest of them all). Ten thousand turkey chicks
Huddled in like barberries shook down from their twigs
After a great storm in the big gray barn. Those that could still
Stand were struggling to come closer to the tin-red heat lamp
That is Mother to us all.
                              Warm (she is), long gone.
The fixed gaze of a barn owl,

                    Or Copernicus, thinking in his age,
Of a kind of brooding between the fixed stars and real life.
I wash the same slice of pear over and over again, the homeliest,
Most mottled one which tastes more tart.
                              Clip-winged, unbeaked,
Take refuge by the heat, the scald of thought, made most magical
For those, in dark, who find their own way by the light of others' eyes.

Eight Takes of Trakl as Himself

I. OF THAT WHICH MAKES A CHILD BLANCH IN SLEEP

          Frost voluptuous, put down
Too early, eavesdrop on the bell tolls, mignonettes.
          What is it that compels you to linger
In the precincts of the hours
          When domesticated creatures
Well know how, by heart, to sleep.
          Silver-fishing; household gods.

II. ACQUISITION OF THE PRONOUN I

          He was bashful as Li Po reaching
From his butter-colored boat to touch
The smudge of moon, eventually. Gloom
                    Is prearticulate.

III. DEMENTIA PRAECOX

Aged five, found unconscious
          In a pile of snow on a bowler-hat-
Shaped hill outside of Salzburg. Half frozen
In the heap of it. The other half his sister,
          Margarethe, her hair the dark plain
Of a harpsichord, her face an autumn day so brazen
It is gold.   Apprentice apples ripen in an azure bowl.

IV. THE QUIET GOD CLOSE HIS BLUE EYES OVER HIM

          His wish to cast himself
Where chestnut-colored horses
          Raised their hooves against the sky.

V. TO THE STARS, A PHYSIOGNOMY

He had never read the face of any soul.
         The mouth a dim albino light.
The eye, to him, an apothecary jar
         Splayed by silver implements.
Stars are maiden-monks in churchyards at Saint Peter's,
         Led by wild wishing-wolves back home.

VI. ALWAYS THE SELF WILL BE BLACK AND NEAR

         A sister's ruddy skirt rustles like a cave
Entered for the first time by a humankind.
He was in love with her. Such as it is to live in the same
         Room with in- and un-intended deaths.
As a sleepwalker, he was precocious, pricked
         With constant pharmaceuticals.

VII. THE WHITE ANGEL

         What is it that compels you
To rearrange the blown-glass bottles
         In the windows of a dusking hall.
Cyanine, half-born; his own father was not his own.
Green, the land of goats extinguishing
         The cool rooms of a hospital.
Red barges floating on the tips of madder ponds.
Amber, a semblance of the ancient Chinese poet, face-down
         In the plough of sallow reeds at night.

         Of the dear dead, how beautiful
It was to walk in the misbegotten shadows
         Of the chalk deer
         Huddle-grazing
In the frisk of misbelief,
            By day, with you.

JUST-SO STORY

I was at home under the shade of the gumbo-limbo tree
Reading the story of what happened to the little elephant with unbridled

Curiosity. Still, I ask too many questions, even now.

I was imagining the common turtle on his Lucite island
In the hollow of the claw-foot tub in our attic dying off with

Little drama all that summer long, the water getting imperceptibly

More shallow every day, while I was riding brindled horses
Up the mountains in the West. I wouldn't know the day he stopped.

It didn't hurt, they told me; he just went to sleep in sun.

I stopped loving a boy one day, which day, exactly,
I wouldn't know, much the same as the never-knowing

When or how the trout I caught regrew the wound

His inner cheek took on (I was groomed to throw him back)
After the whisking of the treble hook went in,

And was then yanked out. Or what hour it could have been
When once my father was at peace,

Alive, wading with me, knee-high into Slippery Rock,

And I stood there with him in the middle of the creek

Curious in wild sun and wondering.

SLEEKER, CURRIER

                         The hides hang in the odd
Two-dimensional shapes of the animal they once were.

Sow, in a rucksack, unfolded, now in the shape of a dull
Ache or a continent, flattened like a blotch of hollyhocks

                         On a fifteenth-century shield. Clove-
Pink, be kind: a mercy is wrapped in a scarf made of autopsy

                         And hoodwinking. A bull
In the shape of his meadow, clovering, incarnate, coming home.

You will not be there, will you now?
                         A satchel of black cherries

Over-ripening in a skirmish of anatomies, puckering
Like the soft spikes of the currycomb. Then groveling,

                         Grooming the animal, even sleeker for the ride.

MENTAL MUSEUM

There is no getting around the gun
In your mouth and the aftermath, a vast migration of stem cells
(We could become—anything—a membrane, a clean new
Set of lungs, whole heart, an artery to replace the one
That had toughened) that could have grown into
A crop of mauve scars, the lot
Of us, broken at the throat, bowered in the ink
Of last speaking, less pink against the paler walls—with this,
You have made of us a scruffy tribe.
Beautiful bright weapons
In the Novembering,   Without you I am even fewer, less.
What an unlikely trundle you have left of
The two beds of the sky.
Pray I
Will be seeing you again, you
Bus-bound for some other country to be alive to die in, just
Not—here, in the roses and bitumen, the corrugated voices of such
Widow-murmuring, where the tenor, too large for good
Health, appeared on the last night of the year, alone on the snow-
Covered hill to sing.
The bindweed
Has no stairway to climb up to—
Look—in this one glass case, a breathless history
Of the unthinkable, each artifact
In the shape of a night-finding bluff or
A species that had never been named,
Sewn up by scars,   Trafficking in salt, as I have.

SILENTIUM

In hospital how high the heat for amaryllis to push out from the furrow of its soil,
Unbroken as a child fleece-bound, making every Ashkenazi angel red in snow.
A microscopic scene of what might have been—if one chromosome
Had misshapen differently. Behind the crescent of the curtain "C,"
A meadow of some suffering, but quietly. Blue-eyed, my wilder gift,
All afternoon the toy wolves have been feeding, almost invisibly it seems.
The marrow of the reeds of wood-wind taps the windowsill. Brother, love as if
I couldn't know that this is bliss—where I am now, the frost so terminal
I keep it in a teacup-tundra lit by cures of cream and unrelieved oblivion.

A Girl's Will

I.

In the garden's bowl of sugar, a company of bees is circling me.
                              They have my back—not stinging,

In the shape of Isadora's scarves in August wind.

II.

                    Such a long time gone for anyone to find me here.

III.

Come to the crinoline fields with me, and fold.
I lay down there once, quite alone,

                              In the oval shape of a Vague.

IV.

It is true, for example, that Miss Duncan kept her protégées (her
          Isadorables) tucked in her own school of silk, batiste, and hurrying,

                    Where pique unfolded boundlessly, i.e., the dead

V.

Don't quarrel and will listen, finally, to Lucie now—still scribbling
Beneath her white uncorseted umbrella in the first draft of an early fall.

The Story of Fraulein X

Where one last late-blooming bird

Sings in the Empress tree.

Where the hens lay

Their eggs without effort and cannot blink.

What is it they are thinking of?

I would not marry to you

Me—bedeviled as a fig tree bound

By burlaps for the winter,

All its branches and their thrushes braided

In and strapped by frost and willfulness

Like a patient run amok

Whose limbs are swaddled

By their endless canvas sleeves

In an aching sack of self.

Such beelzebubbery!

Why is it I didn't love at least

        Not living things.

GREAT RECKONING IN A LITTLE ROOM

All the colors of the trammeled covers in a bed of opium.

The sheen of this, blood-loved as the wound in the haunch of a panther

Downed in an asylum of his own. No, there were no keepers there.

Yes, I am dissembling. In Sweden, the room to put you down was dim,

Candles of no-color held in brown sand-bottomed bags, lit

Like the crooked path on the way to an old sacrarium. After the offering

In a hammered copper bowl filled with big black grapes, I will let you go.

When I say yes, the streetlamp's cylinder of light will come into the room.

It is the last light you will ever stand inside the perfect circle of.

Swallow swallow, deep as the skirts of lingonberries brambling in a blacker forest

And shallow, shallow, you will lay you down.

Uncollected Poem

There should be one spectacular of ruin, red, mid-tragedy.

In Normandy, in the common orchard,
A monk is born into a bottle made of mercury,

Spliced onto a single plum tree twig,

And lives inside the blown glass
                      He grew up into.

                      Dovetail two
Unlikely dreams. Unfold for me but do not leave me

Wise, or full. Do not leave me knowing, known.

Speak to me, not with the meekness of your middle years
                      Or with the mildness

Of a small-brained animal   On its way to abbatoir.

Let me: marrow, let me not   Know exquisite things—

Reveal your form, illusion

Stay—a cut sewn up by the quartet of sad-stringed

Instruments made of cat-gut ligatures still used
                      In certain open-hearted surgeries.

GOULDIAN KIT

What makes you think I'm an eccentric, he said, in London
To the brood of the reporters who had gathered to report

On his eccentricities—the tin sink light enough for traveling
But deep enough to swallow his exquisite hands in water filled with ice.

A budgerigar accompanies, perched atop the fugue of Hindemith.

        You are quivering now like the librarian reading
        To herself out loud in her Arctic room

Composed entirely of snow.

A broadcast (high fidelity) bound by the quiet of the land and
The Mennonite who told him

        We are in this world, but are not of this world,

You see. From the notebook of your partial list of symptoms, phobias:

Fever, paranoia, polio (subclinical), ankle-foot phenomenon,
The possibility of bluish spots. Everything one does is fear

Not being of this world or in this world enough.

        There is no world I know, without some word of it.

OF RICKEY RAY RECTOR

I. AMENDMENT SIX

If you expect this story to be in tact you shouldn't have that
Faith in faith, not here, or in a loping place
Where Rickey Ray won't be so frightened by the dark in Arkansas.

A folk's story of unanswerable griefs—he told me
You will probably not see me anymore after I went home.

Already what was left of him
Was like a barncat leaving just the heart of it, the offering.

II. *STAFF PERSONNEL REPORT JAN 22, 1992*

inmate Rector reports guards are setting loose chickens in the holding cell

pork patty turnips jello muffins milk
pudding—says saving, for just before lights out
reports assorted characters are peering in his window by the towers light

Enough of possim and their teeth, the gold shag's carpeting,

The chinaberry tree back home.   inmate making holling sound

III. THE PORTABLE BAPTISTRY

For you who was taking this down for him, he is all kind about his feeling
For you, you all dressed up like scarecrows   Taken down by other birds.

In the Polaroid he is to his waist in water, plumpened,
Sitting huge and humped up forward, dazy, grinning wide.
This day shall you be with me in paradise.

IV. *STAFF PERSONNEL REPORT JANUARY 23*

inmate glimpses limousine cruising thru prison   all those
he maybe hurt are huddled in the backseat there

6:46 AM   howling
7:07 AM   howling and dancing in cell

8:10, & thruout day   barking while sitting on bunk
began noice's with his voice like a dog

Years after her death, he told me, Mother visits him at night
In her tulip dress, clutching her crocodile pocketbook.

V. ON CLEMENCY

Miss Flowers, he said, Not to worry I'm still voting for your man Miss Gennifer.

Governor Clinton, in his mansion on that last frost night, from time to time
Was having hard time catching breath
Some say
                You will be sleeping when you die.

VI.

How cold that ice cream fell going down.
They is my good ice cream, he said.

VII.

Touches hands of his sisters, first time without glass
—*from Ledger, Visitation House*

A silver canopy over the enormous Elm of him.

VIII. *DEATH-WATCH LOG JANUARY 24*

one steak real done
fried chicken w/ heavy gravy
brown beans three rolls
koolaid, cherry   & he said,   for later—
pecan pie   for just after when he would went to sleep

IX. *from the other side*

Rows of folding chairs unfold, a brood of heavy winter coats settling in
Assembly for the witnessing, like pigeons   Nurse in quiet shoes
Attending with sickness bags
Then a streak of gold light visible through the top of chamber
Where he is   You can hear him helping out

X. *from the other side*

Velvety curtains for the viewing room pulled back,   tell them
Pastor Motton, what it was like the vast bulk   of Rickey Ray
Still bound in with straps of blue still breathing   the lump
Of gauze holds in his fist   his heart's
Green light still   fluttering
Pie still waiting where   he left it there

XI. A LOT SEES—BUT ONLY A FEW KNOWS

I love you Mother in your queen Anne's chair
Geraldo thank you for your company on TV
Bird of prey, waiting like a hearse outside when I'm alive

Salt Lick in Snow

That you would, one day, stop breathing before

My own breath was held.

Were I to wake, muffled through the balsam
Woods, scent of myrrh and mineral.

Would that be tonight.

That we had conducted ourselves with no austerity all along.
Nearer then, a child was a child herself, thin thing

Offering a teaspoonful of civet to the likes

Of us. Beneath the low sky lowering, unclear this time
Of year, you cannot tell

The salt lick from the pale and mackerel

Air around it. That I did not promise. I will never sleep.

MOON RIVER

What is it exactly that you mean when you call me
Your "huckleberry friend"?

                       What if soon you, too, will go down
Like a sheepdog who has tasted blood on a gentleman's farm

Far outside the coal belt, and I do not get to see your
Inflorescence one more time, what then?

Like a lantern-boat half on fire somewhere down
                               The crazy river of your mind,
Framed by endless strings of small whortleberry lights, ablaze,

Still, I go on crossing you in style. My affection has always
Had its girdled caveats—
                    A mushroom-colored cummerbund sashing

The waist of another man, or my feeling formal knowing
When to take the fork out of the toaster, at the very moment of

The metaled tines contacting the one electric outlet in the barn.

Even though you will not speak to me again, not in this life,

Where fear accompanies you like a yellow buggy or a carnivore
With dark spots and a long-ringed tail

                  Unhitched to anything,
                  I forgive you—everything.
                                     Besides,
You've always been such an odd uncanny half-genet of man.

Observations from the Glasgow Coma Scale

Eye Opening in Response to Pain

> Doctor, for the longest spell,

I was bordering on the inexorably humane, of a sudden—
A conspiracy of grace.
> Whole summer in a blaze of gods.

Persistent Inappropriate Speech

Not so much nattering please, says the impresario,
The nurse's commandant on call.
> Still others mumbling
About salted beans left soaking in brisket pots

At home. Some olden Jews are still compelled to hide
Their jewels in smallish alligator carry-ons.

Does Not Open Eyes

A Weimaraner with its two invalid back legs
Tucked in a wheelbarrow rolls down the Avenue Calais.

His master pulls at this contraption with a leash.

Were I to wake
I would not be sanguine if my own hind legs were nulled.

SMILES OR COOS APPROPRIATELY

I was the center of my Mother's world the moment I discovered she could die.

LOCALIZES TO PAIN

A half a century ago, the Nanny kicked our cocker spaniel,
Waldo, down the basement stairs, repeatedly.
When we cannot find the puppy we are told
The creature went, instead, to live the good life
                    On a skein of land they called "a Farm."

CRIES, BUT IS CONSOLABLE

I believe that he was safe there. I am consoled.

The gravestone on my plot in rural Pennsylvania reads:

She Couldn't Help It, Pals

INAPPROPRIATE RESPONSES, WORDS DISCERNIBLE

The heavy rains have been quite excellent for my composure.
I compose myself again in heavy rain.

The trees, stick-figuring, define the view from here.
The waves
                    Are pathographical, disquieting.

Ruby Garnett's Ornament, circa 1892

See, how she tucked her tiny spectacle,
A songbird, behind the chimney bricks

And sealed it shut inside her frayed blue purse,
Some silk grief ago

              Against the indigo of company.

She wrapped his lemon-feathered form
In soft strips of newspaper wetted down

With powdered milk, gentle not to bend a wing
Or break a brittle claw. Her mummery.

In the Dumas Brothel Museum,

In your glass case now, canary, in your
Tin can purged of all its minerals,

You are beautiful, grotesque. I am in this

              Freight and keep myself.
I write home from Butte in mercury.

I take it back from you.   I am on my one.

THREE MEMORIES OF HEAVEN

FIRST MEMORY

It was before the harp, before rain or words

                Before the ox waking in ice.
Before the great warmth turned down in the granaries.
Before the women carding the wool by its temperaments,
Spinning the flaxes away from the rusts, in the valley
Of the stitching in the dresses they will wear tonight.

SECOND MEMORY

Almost like a bird that knows it's about to be born

Before the cut of cinnamon or the linnet-colored
Birthmarks marking with tarnish-scissors even paler things.
It was before I placed my body next to yours, longbone
           To longbone making a kind
Of love that never curdled like the milk at mouths of caves.

It was a time when wren-boys
                Were allowed (out loud) to cry.

THIRD MEMORY

It was all before the bleating or the tears

That I knew the animal must know, before his mistress does—
When she will cut the path toward where he is,
Must know the scent her footprints leave in straw
Must know no heaven, even if it's there in its saffron
Slice, circled with thimbleberries, quick-silvering.
                                        Put your hands
Into the sheets and tell me where the needles are.

RED THREAD

Ash-home. Sack of delicious apples.

Roof of mouth is keen but quiet now.

How is it I did not know the swath
Of you, rare, more rare.

Whole family decimated
                           As if in war.

Old wheat, color of ransack or curlew,
Jews wandering, coppering, each

In their croft. The pond, iced-over now,

Thinner yet for skating. Inside, a man
In his smoking jacket, smoking,

Withholding. Silvering of hair, most

Exigent of needs. In a vase, the red dust

Of gillyflowers aslant by the bed.
Thou shalt not be dead.

                         Last hour
Loving was the first one,

Cruciate as the wings of a dragonfly, at rest.

Death, XXL

                                        Wisdom is ruin.

Dispatch in white chalk left out in the summer rain.

        He is not gone, I asked.

Once (and this was long ago) in the cortège, milkmen wore their folding caps

        And took them off, and workers bent their heads to bow.

The train passed slowly through every belt we know: Prayer, Tornado, Bible, Grain.

No matter what time it was, I will go on missing you again.

In your paddock you were folded like a carriage horse grown too large for his stall.

        Also, there were no carriages left.

Please to find a goddamn other noun. Lie down in it; stay here.

As a young boy, some said, you had once been in heaven, a moment's visit

Through a locked door constructed for the nonce.

Escutcheon in the shape of a boy in the Sun belt, holster round his narrow hips.

      Two tin guns. Ephemera.

Villagers, wallflowers all, huddle under cotton quilts splotched with bougainvillea.

        Here, come trespassing.

Prayer and Amen. Transistor radio.

He is not gone, I asked. *Shot self.* My love.

In the Rust belt, sleep deranges, rearranging our sister's darker rooms.

In the sheepfold, the maid extinguishes her harp, puts her fingers in the felt glove

      Of a persistent vegetative state.

LITTLE INDUSTRY OF GHOSTS

How is it you can explain their living here with me, leaning
On their cellos, doleful and plenty.

In my single person tax-bracket of one alive, there are more
Living here with me not alive

Than are. You are a good
Dog now. Rising, supposing, loom large for me.

Turn down all the rows of white sheets in the rows
Of white cots for your wounded

To settle in. Look, the boy with a cane walks

Three-legged down our Avenue, three-quarters
Of a cur, but he's as gifted limping as the elegy you wrote

For me and I am still alive! It was a poem clear, here
In hindsight, as flounder flesh unwrapped from

Its bed of newspaper, unspoiled. Would that you come home
Now, healed and appalled.

It could have been reparable; we would have gathered
Like a din of two nurses at the metal rails of vigil

At your impossible bed. Would that we, erstwhile, will.
                    Would that our Liam were living still.

Scarinish, Minginish, Griminish

You will not be a sepia hound in my dream at Trotternish, even
      One more time. Not a lighthouse keeper

Landlocked in at Insch, not the deep sea diver with the metal
      Brain in the icy umbraged waters of the Outer Hebrides.

Not at the Firth of Lorne, where each man downed is a tricycle
      Turned over, most of his spokes blown off, not even, were

You luckier, in the heap of small black mussels
      Washed up on the Isle of Skye, huddling but still whole.

You will come back as a starfish, two arms lopped off,

Scooped up by the mop-topped schoolboy, Fearghas,
      Who will take you home to Dingwall when the blotted tide is low,

Collect you with his blush balloons, his tin Sienna soldiers,
      Coloring your endoskeleton with a spot of Maize and Timberwolf

From his set of crayons, flattering you with a Thistle touch, then some
      Dandelion flourishes until his suppertime, one last last dab of Fern—

After which he will go on to his maroon arithmetic and Dostoyevsky
      And his other sullen Prussian Blue and Orchid arts.

THE MATADOR

The last I saw of him was on the final neurasthenic afternoon of his harmonica
When he lost his hair and said I did this to him with my grief,

As the pink halo of a monk's scalp began to shine up through his own.
My grief can cause male-pattern baldness in a man!

        This was his voyage, remember now, not mine.

In my own life's journey, I once found him, many laters, bewitched

Into a tiny iron matador (he wore a hat) on the folding table at a yard sale
In a small New England town, holding out

        His midge of scarf—ridiculous and red,

Now overwrought with aching from the wind in Spain.
              When was it that you say I knew?

Dove, Abiding

I have heard

That you were living like a goat in solitude
And turning in the proxy and the mud of it.

Don't be coy with me. You

Were mean and you were plump. Dove,
Mistaken. You are not good. Heart

The color of a tray of entrails in a Harlem shop

For meats. I have heard Miss X has had a vision
In her rooms. It was uncomely,

A mess of hungry colors, like the Rockettes

Singularly beautiful but all together hideous.
There is no single flower that is not singularly

Beautiful I've heard. I have heard you did not care
For me. You were well-propped in your Tudor

Bed, surrounded by dark
German chocolates, in the tantrum of

Your convalescence that went on and on, though
No one was permitted to know the nature

Of your wound. I have heard
There will be war. Dove mistaken for an abject churl.

I've heard you've set up housekeeping in a factory

For brooms. You do not sweep.

I've heard pink underwings of prior
Wives will not be welcome in your home,

Like spores. I have heard you do go on.

A GIRL AGO

No feeding on wisteria. No pitch-burner traipsing
In the nettled woods. No milk in metal cylinders, no
Buttering. No making small contusions on the page
But saying nothing no one has not said before.
No milkweed blown across your pony-coat, no burrs.
No scent of juniper on your Jacobean mouth. No crush
Of ink or injury, no lacerating wish.
                               Extinguish me from this.
I was sixteen for twenty years. By September I will be a ghost
And flickering in unison with all the other fireflies in Appalachia,
Blinking in the swarm of it, and all at once, above
And on a bare branch in a shepherd's sky.   No Dove.
                         There is no thou to speak of.

Two Girls Ago

No exquisite instruments.

No dead coming back as wrens in rooms at dawn.

No suicidal hankering; no hankering for suicide.

No one thousand days.

No slim luck for the only President I ever loved.

No lukewarm bath in oatmeal.

No lantern left for Natalie on the way home from school in her Alaskan dark.

No eye.

No Victorian slippers that walked the bogs to moor.

No Donner bones with cuts on them or not.

No horizontal weeping; no weeping vertically.

No flipping back your black tails at the black piano bench.

No Elgar, no Tallis, no post-industrial despair.

No French kissing in the field of wild raspberry and thorn.

No commissioned urn.

No threat. In the table of contents I'm not dead yet.

GAUDY INFINITESIMAL

By morning, you will be invisible, mon dream—

You are every rush-moth in your story, every torso, every bitch.

Now, you are distracting Moi.

This is my work, the infidelities of me, my own ivory hillocks, my toy

Pram filled with slippery mice, my own mares fetlock-deep in squalls

Of snow. This was at a time when certain vocables were wearing

Out, torn from being said too much.

When you come home again, each slightly lamed creature will gather

At our garden door. If I listen hard I'll hear the unsewn

Stitching of their improbable and awkward gaits, each one

A little wobbly from the cruelty of the husbandry; your will be done.

Hello Babies, Welcome to Earth

At the theme park in Homestead, past the steel mills along the Allegheny River's

Crinkled bank, I went back home to see if I could grok the way the children

Felt about the Hurdy Gurdy Man, his lugubrious sweet music,

His little capuchin with pin-striped train conductor's cap, held out.

It was a time in the world that was the snowball's one last season on its way to Hell.

The earth loved us a little, I remember, said the note pinned in the seersuckered

Left breast pocket of the Surrealist's suit, on his way to Cincinnati then, by rail.

Small chippy dogs would follow him; he carried bones of milk and scrap.

Only some of us have opposing thumbs but not to worry now.

Poppet, if you've anything to say, you should say it soon I think.

IV

Bird, Singing

Then, every letter opened was an oyster
Of possible bad news, pried apart to reveal

The imperfect probable pearl of your death.

Then, urgent messages still affrighted me, sharp
Noises caused the birds not yet in flight to fly.

Then, this was the life of you.
All your molecules

Gathered for your dying off
Like mollusks clinging to a great ship's hull.

Ceremony of wounds, tinned,
Tiny swaddled starlings soaked in brine.

A bird, singing in his wicker cage, winds down.

Now, a trestle table lined with wooden platters
Neat with feathered wings of quail tucked-in.

Until you sever the thing, from self, it feels.
Thereafter it belongs to none.

You have nothing to be afraid of, anymore.

Outside Prague, I find you warm

Among the million small gold bees set loose
In April's onion snow, quietly

Quietly, would you sing this back to me, out loud?

THE PIANIST

Ivory sailcloth of the nuptial bed, the last fantasia, pulsing, lit.

I was besotted with the fever of the setting free.

Feedbag of meal, the *feeling* of oats, so soft at the muzzle of me.

Then they moved me to a sow-shaped exurb; I did not prosper there.

If you would leave at daybreak, by night I'd wait for you, at everywhere.

                    Your licensed massage therapist

Loves you more concretely than I do. I, abstract, adoring, distant

And unsalvageable. She said, Give up, be palpable—all Hand.

I took to the tawny river and swam into the theater

                    Of the darkened chamber music hall.

                    I loved with all my heart my fear.

You were just an hallucination on my own slow way to sea.

                    On the common, there were swans

Pretending to be boats that carried people

                    Who imagined they felt joy.

ON HAVING CONTRACTED THE HABIT
OF BELIEVING IN THE INTERIOR WORLD

In perpetuity, a basin of water, light, shuddering with its own
Extravagance, gone dull from keeping constant company with relentlessness.

By north, this was when thinking was dwindling and the economy was scarce.

By south, in heat, aluminum buckets of cholera fed to a colony of children
In the camps, those who don't own shoes or roofs or relatives.

The less the light the more the discontent in dark.
                              Inside a mango candle burns all night.

An apparition bunched: the cholera slops in pails from bed to bed, sickling
On one child at a time.

                              If the water had been potable, so easily—
What more is it that you never would have wished for than this is?

Figs ripen from the inside out the way a living patient does and dies.
                              You deserve a better luck than this.

Attitude of Lion

I.

One leaned his beautiful face against the wrought-iron cage and
          Did not give in.

II.

When he was mythic, they combed the mane of him
In the shapes
                    Of spruce lutes from a middle century.
He is still an immortelle,
                    Yellow, numbed, and numinous.

III.

                    Home is the curdled theater where I'm safe.

IV.

He was the smallest in the litter, the mackerel tabby found
By me at the radiator's silver foot, but he was dormant, cold.
Thus began the business about "the Hair," etc., the suicides—

V.

Sejant, I was implacable at the hill's crest not willing
          To go down. The needle and its kind of mercy
Then the tumbling from the furrowed height

VI.

        Into the Dutch elm leaves, a racket of lace,

Then rolling on the wood cart with the cloud-blue wooden wheels, away.

        Couchant, you could stand for a King.

VII.

Your kind, in the oldest British Empire, held up your claws
But you did not roar, not rampantly.

On which continent do your antelopes live still, somewhere grazing
Elegant on red-oat and acacia grass,

VIII.

        Puffed up so as not to look so slender
Or too frail to the more salient hunters of your kind.
I am like you, eyes closed, head low, resting on forepaws as if
                  In sleep, as if asleep.

CONSIDERING THE POSSIBLE MUSIC
OF YOUR HAIR

And all that night carries soundlessly, a satchel of eels.
Fever going down like anemones too full with sweat to float,

Cloak of many blankets wounding you to warmth. It was not,
We both agreed, the time for hospital, its open sea of urgent

Care. Close your eyes and try to sleep. Underwater the music

Of your hair is glossy even now, willowing in currents, away
From our island rancid with the spring.

        Not much longer now.

Green length of one hour, all the blood rushing to the places it will
Not be needed anymore. Now no longer now.

Bramble of needles taken out, for good. So many women
Have run their fingers (as I have) through the glossing of

Your hair—a dormant harp made musical By hand.

FAME RABIES

You are in a sulk, the kinky-bitter
Of frisée smothered by acute
Rosemary, irrevocable sage.

You revile herbs, ambition, fawnery.
Why were you a recluse
Hiding hither, there

In the straw-filled cages
Of the puppy mills,
Waiting there for what.

In the story, your life was young,
Would last. In the east you made
No memories. In the west you never were.

In the middle of the country, once
In a large, aspiring, opaqued crowd,
You could barely wait to be visible.

In two thousand years, malaise
And foaming, hydrophobia—
The diagnosis is not possible

Before the Posthumous. Don't pout.
          What animal, do you think,
Would velvet be the pelt of?

LUCID INTERVAL

Outside the Opera House tonight, in Paris,
A man imagines things, makes wishes
                    Into voices that can sing.
How high the wind is now.
It could not be bitterer than this is.
                    I *am* being here, right now.

I lend to him my hair.
                    Far north of this country,
A castrato who lied about killing a swan—still able
        To fly—was, himself ever after,
Unable to take flight or take to anything at all
                    That sings or glitters, intermittently.

THE ILLUMINATED KUNITZ

Of his early years, scarecrowish at the oval open of the woods,

Both arms outstretched, the cloud-owl began its perching on his clavicle, whoing

Inconstant through that night. This was in the time

Of flannel sleep, the briefer winterlife before this one.

Frost on the window in the shape of interrupted gulls.

White linens folded to be blued and ironed.

Stanley, druid, nobody's daddy but your own—small child, night-gowned

In the backseat of the Buick perching toward the front, asking every

Fourteen miles—*How long till we get home?*—through Pennsylvania Dutch

Land, across the wold of sea, past Willan's Farm where Blake

Had wandered as a boy looking for a chowder-mug of fresh white milk.

In the small illuminations of his work, he tamed the owl: it settled into him,

He said. The child was climbing up the lean celestial ladder,

Minute, particular to her own idea of moon. (She wants she wants she wants.)

We Have Always Lived in the Castle

It was always autumn in the paraphernalia of my laudanums.

There was someone in my autumns in a wheelchair whom my heart

Was aching for—inevitable as moss; the intensity of my sympathy

Was mostly out of fear of living in a chair like that myself.

>   *Wouldn't you feel likewise, if you couldn't—poppet—walk?*

When I was a minx, I always slept alone from him.

Now most everyone *wants* to ask me if I really sleep

And if I love. If they are gentlepersons they shut up.

>   *Indelible,* my joy.

At evening, syrinx of birdsong, obsessive as the woman in the druid-blue

Uniform of a civil servant writing and rewriting marginalia

To the memoir of the life she wished she'd lived.

Of my own venatic arts, everything I ever killed had never been alive.

Then there's the incessant scrubbing of the sugarbowl for arsenic, and guile,

After any hope of fact, forensically.

>   *I'm not bored yet.*

>   And all the dark I did is done.

Medieval Warm Time

Before the Iron Curtain, before the sadder
Century, the one I was born into as
A little Cosmonaut, creeping in bomb shelters
With Mr. White, the school custodian
Who shoveled the coal while I occupied the alcove
Of my ways, it was so warm inside.
That ice age was a little one, a few hundred years about
One thousand years ago. That was all before buttons
And their holes had been considered closure,
Before there was a left shoe from the right.
My mother's hair was ginger-colored, somewhere where
                    It's even colder than it will ever be again.
Everything I ever wished for—
A Dalmatian bounding spotted through the snow.

Cave Painting of a Dun Horse

He is stretching on the wall, appears to be in motion.
He cannot turn his head, but you can glean his eye

By candlelight, a catastrophe of ochre hope.

I know little else having shook loose from my own mane
All that would be true if I said it to be so.

White canes humble through the night.

In the years, most of what I made I made up.

The etching of your dying is as cutting as it was
That many years ago, when I chose its acid touch for you.

There have been two wars.

I have read religiously, mostly texts which have red spines.

I had dreams that were inhumane to me.

The smaller the light to write to becomes, the more
I have to say to you.

Mandelstam

The night calves a meager bit of meat, measured in kilos, from the suddenly bright hay.

Your sadness is a thimble wrapped in a tiny tourniquet by the gauze

Once woven on an inch-loom during a proclamation of great love.

In the Saint Petersburg beneath Saint Petersburg, it is twilight all the time.

Robes so heavy with the heft of snow, such important jewels, no one can move

Without a retinue, a company. Bedouins or wolfhounds beneath stars.

At the sanatorium, your last letter written on a crag of paper asking for warm

Cloth (could it be made?) of cypress light. Even now, it is too cold to be alive.

Heart seized twice, and empathy would make the evening hollow, even by its swathed

And folding wing. Oblivion—a notice to your brother on a green brochure, in time

Arrived by hand to hand to hand.

Non-Fiction Poem

Tonight you wear a jacket lined with the shot silk
Of your early years, color of the silver-dull, Irish farthings

                  In relief of little lyres.

Is it true I will not be here to look after you. What will.

Who will comb your cowlick down?
                         Never-minding the girl of myself

I once ruined, wittingly, with magnolia boughs and willfulness.

                  For example:

My extravagance of gesture;
The maize field fallowed from simplicity; redundancy,

                  The green wind of reckoning.

Did you say I've said "Lark" for the last allotted time?

Have I ever—even once—been disingenuous, not told you

                  Of the truth and nothing but.

CARPE DEMON

Where is your father whose eye you were the apple of?

Where are your mother's parlor portières, her slip-covered days, her petticoats?

In the orchard at the other end of time, you were just a child in ballet slippers,

Your first poodle skirt, your tortoiseshell barrettes. As the peach tree grew more

Scarce each day, you kept running out to try to tape the leaves back on their boughs.

Once, I caught you catch a pond of sunlight in your lap and when you stood,

The sunlight spilt; it could never follow you. Once, above the river,

You told me you were born to be a turtle, swimming down. Under the bridge

Now you take your meals where the thinnest creatures live at the end

Of the world. *Carpe Demon,* you told me just before you put down the phone

And drank the antifreeze. This year, the winter sky in Missouri is a kind of cold

The color of a turtle's hood, a soup of dandelion, burdock root, and clay.

For a Snow Leopard in October

Stay, little ounce, here in
                       Fleece and leaf with me, in the evermore

Where swans trembled in the lake around our bed of hay and morning
Came each morning like a felt cloak billowing

Across the most pale day. It was the color of a steeple disappearing
In an old Venetian sky. Or of a saint tamping the grenadine

Of his heavy robes before the Blessing of the Animals.
I've heard tell of men who brought Great Pyrenees, a borzoi, or

Some pocket mice, baskets of mourning doves beneath their wicker lids,
A chameleon on a leash from the Prussian circuses,

And from the farthest Caucasus, some tundra wolves in pairs.

                                     In a meadow I had fallen

As deep in sleep as a trilobite in the red clay of the centuries.
Even now, just down our winding road, I can hear the children blanketing

Themselves to sleep in leaves from maple trees.
                          No bad dreams will come to them I know

Because once, in the gone-ago, I was a lynx as well, safe as a tiger-iris
In its silt on the banks of the Euphrates, as you were. Would they take

You now from me, like Leonardo's sleeve disappearing in
                       The air. And when I woke I could not wake

You, little sphinx, I could not keep you here with me.
Anywhere, I could not bear to let you go. Stay here

In our clouded bed of wind and timothy with me.

Lie here with me in snow.

A Cage Goes in Search of a Bird

I.

The animals are ironed, docile now, flat at my feet.

II.

I was uncertain of certain mythologies,
Invisible as the milk waiting to happen
To the newborn litter of opossums.

III.

               In a brief violet hour, this time
Of year, the one-winged lapwing tries to fly but stands
Still on the stain of the small accumulation of what was.
Be good, they said, and so too I was
                        Good until I was not.

IV.

It was a time when all the heavens' spare, used vessels coffin-
Cornered down a narrow well of hills, would pour out
To the open sea like a swarm of mourning cloaks, unmuffling.

V.

At the inn, the servants fawn on me. The coachman, vexed,
Treats me as a hummingbird outside its whittled cage.

VI.

An hour in the afternoon of a lark.

VII.

There I slept in the gold folds of the executioner's robe,
All that fabric spilling
Out before him like unbundled honey from its jars.

                                        I am alive
Now. It is the first night of the year. The air is salt
Even this far inland. I wish on a planet, thinking it's a star.
On stars you can wish.

VIII.

There is little left of this, already
Some ilk of lemminglikes
                        Disassemble on the hill.

IX.

It is not volitional.

NOTES

FREEDOM OF SPEECH is for Liam Rector.

The title YOU HAVE HARNESSED YOURSELF RIDICULOUSLY TO THIS WORLD was suggested by a one-line entry (no. 44) in Franz Kafka's "Reflections" collected in his *Blue Octavo Notebooks.*

The poem MEDITATION ON THE SOURCES OF THE CATASTROPHIC IMAGINATION was, in part, suggested by W. G. Sebald's book-length poem, *After Nature.*

Some phrases in OF RICKEY RAY RECTOR are taken from Marshall Frady's "Death in Arkansas" (*The New Yorker,* 22 February 1993). "Staff Personnel Reports" in the poem are quoted from the journals guards kept on death row.

MOON RIVER is for Franz Wright.

Italicized lines in THREE MEMORIES OF HEAVEN are from Rafael Alberti's poem "Three Remembrances of Heaven."

HELLO BABIES, WELCOME TO EARTH is a line from Kurt Vonnegut's 1965 novel, *God Bless You, Mr. Rosewater.*

BIRD, SINGING is for Jason Shinder.

The phrase ON HAVING CONTRACTED THE HABIT OF BELIEVING IN THE INTERIOR WORLD was suggested by Julio Cortázar's poem "Instructions on How to Cry."

CONSIDERING THE POSSIBLE MUSIC OF YOUR HAIR is a phrase adapted from Rafael Alberti's "Three Remembrances of Heaven."

WE HAVE ALWAYS LIVED IN THE CASTLE is the title of Shirley Jackson's final novel, published in 1962.

The title A CAGE GOES IN SEARCH OF A BIRD is adapted from a one-line entry (no. 16) in Franz Kafka's "Reflections" collected in his *Blue Octavo Notebooks.*

Acknowledgments

Selected poems in this work were originally published in the following:

The Academy of American Poets
    "Dove, Interrupted"
    "A Meadow"

The American Poetry Review
    "A Cage Goes in Search of a Bird"
    "Considering the Possible Music of Your Hair"
    "Dear Shadows,"
    "Death, XXL"
    "Dove, Abiding"
    "Fame Rabies"
    "A Girl's Will"
    "Non-Fiction Poem"
    "Of Rickey Ray Rector"
    "Selected Poem"

The Boston Review
    "Bird, Singing"

The Cortland Review
    "Ruby Garnett's Ornament, Circa 1892"

Gulf Coast
    "Little Industry of Ghosts"
    "The Matador"

Lana Turner
    "Of Tookie Williams"

The New Yorker
    "For a Snow Leopard in October"
    "Heat"
    "Infinite Riches in the Smallest Room" (published as "Noctuary")
    "Moon River"

The Paris Review
    "Posthumous Seduction"

Parnassus: Poetry in Review
 "Freedom of Speech"
 "Meditation on the Sources of the Catastrophic Imagination"
 "Notes from the Trepidarium"
 "Observations from the Glasgow Coma Scale"

Poetry Magazine
 "Carpe Demon"
 "Currying the Fallow-Colored Horse"
 "Extreme Wisteria"
 "Father, in Drawer"
 "Gouldian Kit"
 "You Have Harnessed Yourself Ridiculously to This World"

Poetry Salzburg
 "A Girl Ago"
 "Two Girls Ago"

Something Understood: Essays & Poetry for Helen Vendler
 "In Owl Weather"

The New Republic
 "Just-So Story"

A Note About the Author

Lucie Brock-Broido (1956–2018) was the author of several collections of poetry, including *A Hunger, The Master Letters,* and *Trouble in Mind,* and was the editor of *Letters to a Stranger* by Thomas James. *Stay, Illusion,* first published in 2013, was a finalist for the National Book Award. A longtime director of Poetry in the School of the Arts at Columbia University, Brock-Broido was a beloved teacher and the recipient of awards from the John Simon Guggenheim Memorial Foundation, the National Endowment for the Arts, and the American Academy of Arts and Letters.

A Note on the Type

This book was set in Adobe Garamond. Designed for the Adobe Corporation by Robert Slimbach, the fonts are based on first cut by Claude Garamond (c. 1480–1561). We owe to Garamond the type we now know as "old style." He gave to his letters a certain elegance and feeling of movement that won their creator an immediate reputation and the patronage of Francis I of France.

COMPOSED BY NORTH MARKET STREET GRAPHICS, LANCASTER, PENNSYLVANIA
PRINTED AND BOUND BY THOMSON-SHORE, DEXTER, MICHIGAN
DESIGNED BY IRIS WEINSTEIN